Let's Discover the Alef Bet

TEACHING GUIDE

By
Ari Y. Goldberg

Education Consultants
Treasure Cohen
Linda Czuper
Elaine Gaidemak
Dr. Gavriel Goldman

Behrman House, Inc.

Arts and Crafts activities on pages 19 and 28
reprinted with permission by Tracey Cass Agranoff.

Copyright © 1999 by Behrman House, Inc.

Published by Behrman House
West Orange, NJ 07052

www.behrmanhouse.com

ISBN 0-87441-687-6

MANUFACTURED IN THE UNITED STATES OF AMERICA

Table of Contents

INTRODUCTION

The Importance of Hebrew

Beginning to learn Hebrew is an important milestone in a child's Jewish education. The Hebrew language is one of the universal connections among Jews around the world, as well as for countless generations of Jews throughout history. Indeed, Hebrew is not just one of many international languages. Its words represent the moral and ritual teachings of the Jewish people. Most Jews, both children and adults, develop a Hebrew vocabulary without even knowing it. Words such as *Torah, mitzvah, shofar,* and *menorah* have become such an integral part of our Jewish culture and language that we often don't even stop to think that these are Hebrew words.

What's Special About *Let's Discover the Alef Bet*

Let's Discover the Alef Bet provides the necessary structure and materials to introduce children to the Hebrew alphabet. The primary goal of these folders is to create a level of comfort and familiarity with the letters of the Alef Bet, in an entertaining and playful framework. We want the students to "make friends" with the letters. Using the techniques suggested in this Guide, you can teach the name, shape, and sound of each of the 22 Hebrew letters, while introducing the children to a basic Hebrew vocabulary. Teaching Jewish concepts is also an integral part of each folder. Children not only learn Hebrew vocabulary words but will also understand their context within Jewish tradition.

Family Education

Establishing a partnership between home and school helps the Jewish educational experience reach its greatest potential. To facilitate this partnership, each folder concludes with a section entitled "In School or At Home." In addition, at the end of this Guide you will find "Learning at Home"—letters for you to photocopy and send home to encourage family participation. You will also find, under the heading "Family Education Experience," enrichment sheets to be duplicated and sent home to reinforce and expand upon the material in the folders.

When It Is Time to Teach

You may use this Teaching Guide selectively. Each lesson is full of ideas for discussion, activities, and projects. Choose those items with which you feel most comfortable. Keep in mind your teaching style and the makeup of your group. Most important, be creative, be full of surprises, and have fun!

How to Use This Guide

Structure of the Folders

Let's Discover the Alef Bet comprises 24 four-page folders—one folder for each of the 22 letters of the Alef Bet, plus one Review folder and one Family Education folder. Every letter folder contains the following elements:

- A key Hebrew word—with an accompanying picture and an English explanation—to teach the new letter
- Inventive activities to reinforce the shape and sound of each letter
- Additional Hebrew vocabulary words beginning with the new letter
- Playful exercises to engage the child's artistic and creative interests
- "In School or At Home"—an activity to be used in the classroom or sent home to encourage family participation

Purposes of *Let's Discover the Alef Bet*

Introduce the names of the letters of the Hebrew alphabet
Introduce the sounds of the letters
Present the order of the Alef Bet
Develop visual recognition of letter symbols
Develop auditory discrimination of letter sounds
Demonstrate that Hebrew is read from right to left
Develop letter-sound associations
Provide pictorial reinforcement to link letters and sounds
Introduce a primary Hebrew vocabulary

Teaching the Folders

These folders should be taught in order—1 through 23—because many of the letter and word recognition activities are cumulative. (As will be discussed later, Folder 24—A Family Education Folder—should be sent home at the beginning of the school year.) For your convenience, each folder is numbered on the front page at the top left corner under the *Let's Discover the Alef Bet* logo.

Students differ in ability and teachers differ in style. Ultimately, you will have to decide how to pace your class's progress. Many classes will cover one folder per week; some may be able to cover as many as two folders in one week, while others may have to proceed more slowly. Remember that mastery of each new letter, rather than speed, is what is most important.

Scope and Sequence—Letters and Key Words

The words introduced in each lesson will help the children hear and remember the sound of the Hebrew letter being studied. The accompanying pictures provide Hebrew language readiness and offer the opportunity to teach a basic Hebrew vocabulary.

One of the best ways to teach the order of letters in the alphabet is to sing them. Make singing "The Alef Bet Song" an ongoing classroom experience.

Folder	Letter	Key Word	Supplemental Words
1	Alef	alef bet	Aron Kodesh (Holy Ark), aryeh (lion)
2	Bet	bayit (house)	beit knesset (synagogue)
3	Gimmel	glidah (ice cream)	g'vinah (cheese), gamal (camel), galgal (wheel), gezer (carrot)
4	Dalet	degel (flag)	dag (fish)
5	Hay	Havdalah	Haggadah
6	Vav	vered (rose)	
7	Zayin	zebrah (zebra)	
8	Het	hallah	Hanukkah
9	Tet	tallit	Tu B'Shevat
10	Yud	yeladim (children)	yad (hand), yarok (green)
11	Kaf	kelev (dog)	kippah
12	Lamed	lulav	leitsan (clown), lehem (bread), luah (chalkboard), lev (heart)
13	Mem	matzah	mezuzah
14	Nun	ner tamid (eternal light)	ner (candle)
15	Samech	sukkah	sefer (book), soos (horse), sevivon (Hanukkah top)
16	Ayin	etz (tree)	oogah (cake)
17	Pay	parpar (butterfly)	parah (cow), pa'amon (bell), pil (elephant)
18	Tsadee	tsedakah	ts'fardeya (frog)
19	Koof	keshet (rainbow)	Kiddush, kof (monkey)
20	Resh	rimonim	rakevet (train)
21	Shin	shofar	shemesh (sun), shulhan (table), sha'on (clock), Shabbat
22	Tav	Torah	tapoo'ah (apple)

Creating a Hebrew Environment

The appearance of your classroom is an important source of motivation for learning. The classroom should convey the message that Hebrew is exciting, fun, and important. Play recordings of Israeli songs. Hang Alef Bet charts and attractive Hebrew posters around the room. Display a selection of Hebrew books or anything else that contains Hebrew letters. Label classroom objects with their Hebrew names. Try to include items of a religious nature (e.g., a Haggadah, a hallah cover), as well as items from Israeli popular culture (e.g., soda labels, comic books).

Calling students by their Hebrew names is a valuable way to personalize the Hebrew language. Ask students to tell the class their Hebrew name. If they don't know it, have them ask their parents. If a child does not have a given Hebrew name, try finding a Hebrew name that is roughly equivalent to the child's English name. For example, if a child's name is Jonathan, the Hebrew equivalent would be Yonatan.

Structure of the Teaching Guide

This Teaching Guide will help you build upon the material that is in the students' folders. Before teaching a folder in class, read through the teaching suggestions in this Guide to help in preparing your lesson plan. Following are descriptions of the different features you will find in this Guide:

Key Word
The key word in each folder and its definition.

Let's Talk About It
Points to emphasize and questions to ask. May include suggestions on how to use the photographs to enhance the lessons.

Jewish Value
Background information for the teacher about a Jewish value that can be learned from one of the vocabulary words. May also include ideas for teaching the value.

Arts and Crafts
Age-appropriate projects with basic instructions.

Hands-On Activities
Teaching techniques for using the activities in the folders, plus additional suggested activities.

My Family and Me
Home activities to encourage family participation. Some of these activities are also included in the "Learning at Home" send-home letters to parents, which are in Part 2 of this Teaching Guide.

Helpful Hints
Additional information and teaching suggestions. Usually related to teaching the new Hebrew letter.

Supplemental Words
Additional Hebrew words contained in the student folders.

Family Education

Family education is a vital component of *Let's Discover the Alef Bet,* and every effort should be made to facilitate a partnership with your students' families. Each student folder concludes with an activity called "In School or At Home," which can be completed in the classroom or sent home to encourage family participation. In addition, this Teaching Guide contains several other components to promote family education.

- For each of the 23 classroom folders, this Guide provides suggestions for home activities that bolster family participation. These "My Family and Me" suggestions can be found in Part 1.

- This Guide also contains "Family Education Experience" black-line masters for folders 5, 10, and 14 that can be duplicated and sent home to supplement the "My Family and Me" activities in those folders.

- In Part 2 of this Guide you will find seven letters to parents, entitled "Learning at Home." These letters encourage parents to become involved in their children's religious and Hebrew education by updating the parents about the material that has been taught and by suggesting family activities. Duplicate the letters and send them home with the appropriate folders after classroom use.

Teaching Strategies

Teaching the Letter

It is important to keep in mind that people learn in different ways. Therefore, teach each letter in as many ways as possible so that you can reach every child in the class. Following are some methods for teaching the Hebrew letters:

1) Introduce the letter by saying: "This is a Hebrew letter. The name of the letter is _____." Carefully demonstrate how the sound is made. Have the children repeat the name and the sound several times with you.

2) Ask the children to point to the Hebrew letter printed on the first page of the folder. Say the name of the letter, and ask them what sound they think the letter makes. (Remember: The name of the letter usually reinforces the sound that the letter makes.) Have children repeat the name of the letter and its sound several times.

3) Ask the children to trace the letter with their fingers as they repeat the sound of the letter. This will help them to commit the shape and the sound to memory.

4) It is possible to find many of the Hebrew letters in the shape of classroom objects. As a new letter is being learned, have children look around the room to see whether they can find that letter shape. For example, a doorframe makes a perfect Het; some desktops look like Lameds; and Vavs are found everywhere. Children can also do this activity at home with their families.

Using the Key Word

The key word in each folder will help the children hear and remember the sound of the letter being studied. At the same time, the children will have the opportunity to acquire a basic Hebrew vocabulary. You can teach either the letter or the key word first. Feel free to choose whichever option works best for you and your class.

1) Tell the children to look at the picture on the first page of the folder, and teach them the Hebrew word for it. Emphasize the initial sound of the word. Say the Hebrew word for the picture several times, and have the children repeat it after you.

2) Play a guessing game. For example, tell the class that you are thinking of something that begins with the letter *i*. Encourage them to ask questions before they guess the answer: "Is it something to eat...something in the synagogue...a kind of toy?" After they guess the word (ice cream), teach it to them in Hebrew (*glidah*). Then point out the Gimmel and demonstrate its sound.

After introducing the key word and demonstrating its connection to the letter being learned, you can discuss Jewish concepts related to the key word. For example, when teaching the letter Bet and the word *bayit*, you can also introduce the concept of *sh'lom bayit*—keeping peace in the house. Refer to Part 1 of this Teaching Guide (pages 14–36) for information to assist you in discussing these Jewish concepts.

How to Use the Exercises

Each folder contains one or more exercises to practice each new letter or word. Be sure to explain the directions to students and to discuss the purpose of each exercise. The completed example in some exercises shows the students what to do. You may work together with the group on one or two items, but then allow each child to finish the exercise independently. Check that children are working on the activity from right to left.

Review the completed exercise together. Offer plenty of praise for a job well done. If there are errors, give plenty of encouragement by saying things like: "Let's look at this one together. Does this letter look different from the rest? In what way?"

How to Use "In School or At Home"

The final page of each of the letter folders consists of an exercise entitled "In School or At Home." This exercise can be used in the classroom or done at home to encourage family participation. By completing this page at home, students can demonstrate to their parents what they have learned in class.

You may want to consider what other classroom materials are being sent home when deciding whether to do these exercises in school or at home. You may want to alternate—one week in school, next week at home, etc. In addition, you should try to gauge the students' mastery of the material and their ability to complete the exercise without your assistance.

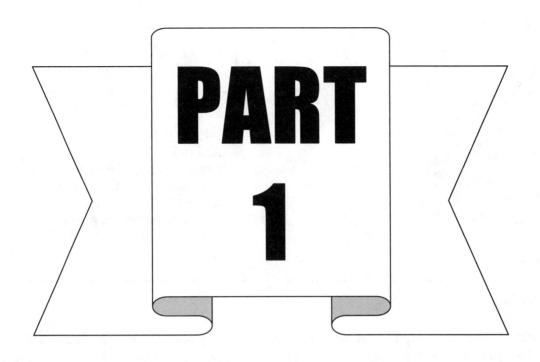

PART
1

HOW TO USE
THE FOLDERS

Don't forget to begin the lesson by teaching the new letter and key word. See pages 11–12 for strategies.

Key Word
Alef Bet
Alef is the name of the first letter in the Hebrew alphabet. The second letter is Bet. That is why the name of the Hebrew alphabet is Alef Bet.

Folder 1

Jewish Value
Joy of Beginning Hebrew Study
The beginning of Hebrew study has always been considered a joyous event in a child's Jewish education. Explain that there is a custom of eating something sweet on the first day of school so that learning will be a sweet and happy experience. Arrange to have candy, raisins, or other sweets to distribute to each child. Consider also having other treats, such as pretzels or popcorn, for students who may have special dietary concerns.

Arts and Crafts
Give each student a manila envelope to store the *Let's Discover the Alef Bet* folders until they are taken home. Have students decorate the envelopes with Jewish symbols.

Hands-On Activities
(A) Do an Alef Bet treasure hunt in the classroom. Print an Alef on pieces of construction paper and hide them throughout the classroom. Consider breaking the class into teams.

(B) Demonstrate how to open a Hebrew book. Ask a student to come up and find the first page in one of the books. What are some clues to finding the front of a book? [e.g., front cover, title page, table of contents] Explain that the folders open like Hebrew books since they teach the Hebrew letters.

My Family and Me
Distribute Folder 24—A Family Education Folder. Explain how the Alef Bet chart and the Hebrew playing cards can be used at home. Make sure that the children understand that they should give this folder to their parents.

Helpful Hints
When teaching the sound of the Alef, tell the students to be very quiet. Then tell them that you will now demonstrate the sound of the Alef. Let the room be totally quiet for a few seconds. Ask whether anyone heard the sound that Alef makes.

Supplemental Words
Aron Kodesh (Holy Ark)

ב
בַּיִת

Folder 2

Don't forget to begin the lesson by teaching the new letter and key word. See pages 11–12 for strategies.

Key Word
Bayit
House

Jewish Value
Sh'lom Bayit (Peace in the House)
Ask the children whether they know what the word *shalom* means. Discuss its various meanings (hello, goodbye, and peace). Introduce the phrase *sh'lom bayit*—"peace in the house." What do the students think it means to have peace in the house? Explain that Judaism teaches that each of us must help to make living in our homes as pleasant as possible. Go around the room and ask students what they can do to help keep *sh'lom bayit* in their homes.

Arts and Crafts
Give children a piece of drawing paper and have them fold it in half. Have them choose one way that they can help keep *sh'lom bayit* in their homes. On the left side, have the children draw a picture of the action they chose. On the right side, have them draw a picture depicting what would happen if they didn't behave in that way. For example, to keep *sh'lom bayit* the child cleans his or her room. If the child didn't do this, the room would be messy. Then there would not be *sh'lom bayit* because the child's parents would be upset that the room had not been cleaned.

Hands-On Activities
Take your students on a tour of the synagogue—the *beit knesset*. Make sure to plan stops at different points along the way. For example, read a story in the library, recite a prayer in the sanctuary, learn an Israeli dance in the social hall, and have a snack in the kitchen. Emphasize how the different activities in the synagogue bring Jews together in the house of meeting (*beit knesset*).

My Family and Me
Talk about what makes a Jewish *bayit* and what makes something a Jewish object. Have the students bring one Jewish object from their *bayit* to the next class session for "show and tell." These can be objects such as a kippah, a Hanukkah menorah, or a Kiddush cup.

Helpful Hints
When teaching the letter Bet, show the students that "**B**et has a **b**elly **b**utton" (the dot).

Supplemental Words
beit knesset (synagogue)

גְּלִידָה

ג

Folder 3

just a **Reminder**

Don't forget to begin the lesson by teaching the new letter and key word. See pages 11–12 for strategies.

Key Word
Glidah
Ice cream

Let's Talk About It

Ask your students to imagine themselves in the photograph and to describe the taste of *glidah* on a hot day. Have them name their favorite flavors of *glidah*. One way to help the children remember the Hebrew word is by going around the room and having them say: "My tongue glides on _____ (fill in flavor) *glidah* when I lick it."

Jewish Value

Brachot (Blessings)

We say a blessing, a *brachah*, before eating to give thanks to God for the food. Discuss why and when we say "thank you" to other people. What are different ways we can say thank you? [e.g., note, flowers, phone call, saying a blessing] Why might we say thank you for something that we do not like, such as a gift? [We should be grateful for the kindness of the person who gave the gift.]

Teach the following blessing that can be said before eating ice cream, and then serve some ice cream as a special treat. Have an alternate treat for those students with special dietary concerns.

Baruch atah, Adonai Eloheinu, melech ha'olam, shehakol nihyeh bidvaro.
Praised are You, Adonai our God, Ruler of the world, at whose word all things come into being.

Arts and Crafts

Ask the children to draw a picture of something that God has created. Then ask them to make up a blessing to thank God for this creation.

Hands-On Activities

Call out different Hebrew words that begin with Alef, Bet, and Gimmel. Tell the children to jump up when you call out a Gimmel word. See folders 1, 2, and 3 for the words that have been learned so far.

My Family and Me

Duplicate the "Learning at Home" letter on page 38 of this Guide. Send the letter and folders 1–3 home with the students.

Supplemental Words

g'vinah (cheese)   gamal (camel)   galgal (wheel)   gezer (carrot)

דֶּגֶל

Folder 4

Don't forget to begin the lesson by teaching the new letter and key word. See pages 11–12 for strategies.

Key Word
Degel
Flag

Let's Talk About It

Have the students name different times and places where they might see a flag. [e.g., in a parade, outside a school, on a holiday] Why do we display and wave flags? [e.g., to feel proud, to show people what is important to us, to represent a group or club to which we belong] How do we usually feel when we are waving a flag? [happy, joyful]

What flags are the girls in the photograph holding? [Israeli flags] What else do you see in the picture? [balloons] Why do you think that they are waving these flags? [It is Yom Ha'atzmaut (Israel Independence Day) or Simhat Torah.] On which holiday do we usually wave flags in the synagogue and why? [On Simhat Torah we celebrate finishing reading the Torah. We are so happy that we sing and parade around the synagogue. We take out the Torah Scrolls from the *Aron Kodesh* and march around the synagogue in a parade called *hakkafot*.]

Jewish Value
Showing Respect for Special Objects

Explain to the students that there are laws about how flags are supposed to be displayed. For example, flags are not supposed to be displayed if it is raining or if the flag is torn. This is done out of respect for the flag. How do we show respect for objects in Judaism, like the Torah or a siddur (prayerbook)? [e.g., kiss a siddur when we drop it, stand when the Torah is taken out of the Ark]

Arts and Crafts

Why does the American flag have fifty stars? [fifty states] Why does an Israeli flag have a *Magen David* (Star of David)? [It is a symbol that represents the Jewish people.] Have the students make their own flag and include things that represent their family. These could include the number of people in their family, pets, something distinctive about their house, hobbies, favorite Jewish symbol or holiday, etc.

My Family and Me

Many families own precious objects that they treat with particular respect. Often these items are family heirlooms. Discuss what an heirloom is. Have the students discuss with their parents whether there is any item in their household that they treat with special respect, and have them ask the reason why.

Supplemental Words

dag (fish)

הַבְדָלָה

Don't forget to begin the lesson by teaching the new letter and key word. See pages 11–12 for strategies.

Key Word
Havdalah
Separation. Ceremony performed on Saturday evening to mark the conclusion of Shabbat.

Folder 5

Let's Talk About It
Look at the photograph on the cover. What is special about the candle? [braided, has multiple wicks] What other Jewish objects are in the picture? [kippah, Kiddush cup, siddur, spice box] What is inside the silver box the boy is smelling? [sweet-smelling spices]

Jewish Value
Havdalah—Separating the Holy from the Ordinary
Explain that Havdalah means "separation." Havdalah separates the holiness and specialness of Shabbat from the ordinariness of the rest of the week. We smell sweet spices to have one last breath of Shabbat sweetness as the week begins. We hold our hands in front of the candle to see that the bright light and the dark shadow on our hands is like the difference between the holiness of Shabbat and the ordinariness of the week. We drink wine to end Shabbat in the same way that we began it.

Arts and Crafts
You can purchase wax sheets in assorted colors that can be cut into 1" x 7" strips. If you put them in hot water, they will become malleable. The children can punch them down, add a wick, fold the wick over inside, and braid using three colors.

Hands-On Activities
Demonstrate and explain the different parts of the Havdalah ceremony.

My Family and Me
Encourage the students and their families to go outside their homes on a Saturday evening and search the sky for three stars. Then they can announce the end of Shabbat with Havdalah. The "Family Education Experience" sheet on page 46 contains the text of the Havdalah service and an explanation; it should be sent home with the "Learning at Home" letter on page 39 after folders 4–6 are completed.

Helpful Hints
When teaching the letter Hay, demonstrate how the sound is made by placing a tissue in front of your mouth. What happens to the tissue when you make the sound? [The tissue is blown outward.]

Supplemental Words
Haggadah

ו

וֶרֶד

Folder 6

Don't forget to begin the lesson by teaching the new letter and key word. See pages 11–12 for strategies.

Key Word
Vered
Rose

Let's Talk About It
Ask the students how they feel when they look at the picture of a rose on the first page of the folder. When might they give someone flowers? [e.g., Mother's Day, to cheer someone up] Explain that we often display flowers because they help to make the room prettier (e.g., at a wedding or party, in a hospital room).

Jewish Value
Protecting the Environment
There is a legend that after the creation of the world, God took Adam and Eve around the Garden of Eden and showed them all of its beauty. God then said to them, "I have created all of this for you. Please take care of it. Do not spoil or destroy My world." This legend teaches us to care for the earth's natural resources. Ask the children what they can do to take care of the world.

Arts and Crafts
Using colored paper and markers, design a face and then glue it onto a styrofoam cup. (Design a face only. No need to make hair.) Fill a second cup three quarters full with potting soil. Sprinkle parsley seeds over the soil and cover them with a little more soil. Pat gently and then water. Once the decorations have dried, place the cup of soil into your decorated cup. Put your plant in a sunny spot. After about 10 days the first sprouts will appear, and your cup will soon grow a full head of green "hair."

My Family and Me
A) Duplicate the "Learning at Home" letter on page 39 of this Guide. Send the letter and folders 4–6 home with the students. Be sure to include the "Family Education Experience" sheet on page 46.

B) A fun activity to do at home is to make a flowerpot filled with "edible dirt." Take a small flowerpot or a large paper cup. Fill it three quarters full with instant chocolate pudding. Place an artificial flower (preferably a *vered!*) in the center, so that it looks like it is growing naturally. Sprinkle Oreo ® cookies, crushed very finely, over the top of the pudding thoroughly, so that the pudding is not visible. The children can trick people into thinking they are eating dirt when they eat a spoonful! You can also say the *shehakol* blessing when eating it (page 16).

זֶבְּרָה

Key Word

Zebrah
Zebra

Folder 7

Jewish Value
There Is a Reason for Everything
Have you ever seen a zebra? Where? Ask the question found in the folder: "Do you think a zebra is white with black stripes, or black with white stripes?" Jews believe that God created everything in the world for a reason. Ask students why they think God might have made zebras look the way they do. [camouflage]

Arts and Crafts
Have the children draw animal faces on oaktag and make masks from the drawings. A string or a rubber band can be used to hold the mask in place. If none of the children makes a zebra mask, the teacher should make one.

Explain that according to the Torah, Adam, the first person, was given the job of naming all the animals. Have the students give new names to the animals that they made.

Hands-On Activities
Divide the class into groups and have a "sing-down." Give each group three minutes to come up with a list of as many animals as they can, but the students must be able to imitate the sounds that the animals make. Then sing "Old McDonald Had a Farm," calling on the groups, one at a time, to supply the next animal on the farm.

My Family and Me
The next time the children go to the zoo with their families, ask them to talk about what makes each animal unique and why they think God created the animals to look as they do. For example, the quills on a porcupine offer protection; gills on fish allow them to breathe underwater.

Helpful Hints
Be sure that the students understand the slight difference in pronunciation of the word *zebrah* in English and Hebrew (ZEE-BRA vs. Zeh-BRAH). Also, ask how the shape of the letter Zayin is different from the letter Vav that they just learned.

ח

חַלָה

Folder 8

Don't forget to begin the lesson by teaching the new letter and key word. See pages 11–12 for strategies.

Hallah
The braided bread that we eat at Shabbat and holiday meals.

Jewish Value
Shabbat as a Day of Rest
Ask the students whether they like to take naps or to go to bed when their parents tell them. Why don't they want to go to sleep? [There are so many things that they want to do.] Without God's example of resting on the seventh day—Shabbat—people might not even know how to rest and relax. God had to create a day of rest because otherwise the world would be a place always "on the go." How would you feel if you never took the time to slow down and rest?

Arts and Crafts
Help the children make hallah covers using cloth or felt and fabric paints. Have them decorate the covers with pictures of objects or scenes related to Shabbat. Prepare a stencil for the children so that they can paint the letter Het on the covers.

Hands-On Activities
Have the students make their own hallah rolls to use on Shabbat. To save time, prepare the dough in advance. Most Jewish cookbooks will have a hallah recipe. (Some bakeries will sell you dough upon request.) Give children a strip of dough and show them how to form a roll. If desired, have appropriate toppings, such as raisins, sesame seeds, and poppy seeds, to sprinkle on top of the rolls.

My Family and Me
Encourage the students to recite the *Hamotzi* blessing over hallah at the beginning of dinner every Friday night. The blessing is on the back page of the folder.

Helpful Hints
If the students have difficulty pronouncing the sound of the letter Het, suggest that the sound is similar to that in "yuch," which they might say when something doesn't taste good. Also, point out the similarities and differences between the letters Het and Hay.

Supplemental Words
Hanukkah

טַלִּית

Folder 9

just a **Reminder** Don't forget to begin the lesson by teaching the new letter and key word. See pages 11–12 for strategies.

Key Word
Tallit
The prayer shawl Jews wear during morning prayer. The fringes on the corners of the tallit are called *tzitzit*.

Jewish Value
Tzitzit Remind Us of the Mitzvot
Bring a tallit to class and let the students touch it and examine it closely. Make sure they pay special attention to the *tzitziyot* (fringes). You can explain that although a tallit is usually white with black or blue stripes, it can be any color.

Demonstrate how a tallit is worn, and explain that it is traditionally worn during morning services. Explain that all *tallitot* (plural of tallit) must have *tzitziyot*, which are made of white threads knotted in a special way to remind us of the 613 *mitzvot* that God gave to the Jewish people.

Ask the students why they think that a tallit is worn. [e.g., to help us concentrate on our prayers; the *tzitzit* remind us to do *mitzvot*—God's commandments] A tallit is not worn until you become a Bar/Bat Mitzvah. What can you do until you become a Bar/Bat Mitzvah to remember to follow the *mitzvot*?

Arts and Crafts
Ask students to name different *mitzvot* that can be done each day. List all the suggestions on the chalkboard. The list could include things such as making a card for someone who is sick, feeding my pet, cleaning my room, and saying the blessing over bread. Have each student choose two of these *mitzvot* to try and observe regularly and then write these two *mitzvot* at the bottom of a piece of drawing paper.

Have the students then write the number 613 in large characters on the drawing paper. Briefly explain that according to Jewish tradition there are 613 *mitzvot* that God gave to the Jewish people. Because this number is unique, every time Jews hear or see the number 613, we should think of the *mitzvot*. Have the children decorate the rest of the drawing paper with Jewish symbols. Make a hole at the bottom right of the paper and tie a piece of string to it. Just as with the *tzitzit* on a tallit, every time the children see the string on this art project, they will be reminded of the *mitzvot* that God has given us.

My Family and Me
Duplicate the "Learning at Home" letter on page 40 of this Guide. Send the letter and folders 7–9 home with the students.

Supplemental Words
Tu B'Shevat

22

ר

יְלָדִים

Folder 10

Don't forget to begin the lesson by teaching the new letter and key word. See pages 11–12 for strategies.

Key Word
Yeladim
Children

Jewish Value
Blessing of Children
Ask the students to list the different rituals that are done as part of Shabbat dinner on Friday night. [Kiddush, lighting candles, blessing over hallah]

Ask the students to name different ways that their parents show that they love them. [e.g., hugs and kisses, saying "I love you," giving presents, taking them places, correcting them when they do something wrong] Explain that a special way for parents to show their love is by reciting a blessing for their children on Shabbat. The parents place their hands on each child's head and then recite: "*May Adonai bless you and guard you. May Adonai show you favor and be gracious to you. May Adonai show you kindness and grant you peace.*"

Arts and Crafts
Tell the children that they are going to use their *yad* to paint a picture. What kind of painting would this be? [finger painting] Using a large piece of newsprint, have each child make a handprint in the middle of the paper. Then have the children finger-paint a design around their handprint. Teach the word *yarok,* and have them use green paint to make the letter Yud in the center of their handprint.

Hands-On Activities
Play "Simon Says" with the students, but use the word *yad* instead of hand when giving instructions. For example, "Put your *yad* on your head."

My Family and Me
The "Family Education Experience" sheet on page 47, which contains the text and a description of the parental blessing over children, should be sent home with the "Learning at Home" letter on page 41 after folders 10–12 are completed. Encourage parents to bless their children as part of the weekly routine.

Helpful Hints
Try to use the word *yeladim* as much as possible during this lesson. For example, you might say, "*Yeladim*, please go to your seats."

Supplemental Words
yad (hand)   yarok (green)

כ

כֶּלֶב

Folder 11

Don't forget to begin the lesson by teaching the new letter and key word. See pages 11–12 for strategies.

Key Word
Kelev
Dog

Jewish Value
Tsa'ar Ba'alei Hayyim (Being Kind to Animals)
Ask whether any of the children have pets. Have them describe what they do to care for the pet. [e.g., feed it, walk it, give it medicine, bathe it, clean up after it] What would happen if you forgot to feed the pet? Can the pet get food for itself? Emphasize the owner's responsibility to care for the pet. Explain that every time they take care of their pets, play with them, take them for walks, or feed them, they are performing the mitzvah of *tsa'ar ba'alei hayyim*—being kind to animals.

Arts and Crafts
Have the students draw a picture of a *kelev*. Have different colors of yarn available for the children to glue onto the *kelev* as fur.

Hand-On Activities
Ask the students to demonstrate different ways that dogs bark (e.g., happy, ferocious, in pain). Just as dogs bark differently for different reasons, so people talk differently when they are happy, scared, or in pain. How should we react when we hear the different types of dog barks? [e.g., play with a dog barking happily, get away from a dog barking ferociously, get help for a dog barking in pain] Each of these reactions shows *tsa'ar ba'alei hayyim*. Being kind to animals doesn't only mean not mistreating animals; it also means treating them with respect when they exhibit different emotions.

My Family and Me
Encourage the students to fulfill the mitzvah of *tsa'ar ba'alei hayyim* with their families by making a bird feeder. Take dried slices of bread and cover them with peanut butter. Press birdseed into the peanut butter and hang the bread slices from a tree limb with a piece of string or ribbon.

Helpful Hints
Because of the similarity in appearance between the letters Kaf and Bet, be sure to discuss how these letters differ. It may help the students to remember that "Kaf is curvy."

Supplemental Words
kippah

לוּלָב

Folder 12

 just a Reminder

Don't forget to begin the lesson by teaching the new letter and key word. See pages 11–12 for strategies.

Key Word
Lulav

The combination of a palm branch, myrtle, and willow leaves, which are bound together and ceremoniously shaken, along with an etrog, on the holiday of Sukkot.

Let's Talk About It

What is the boy in the photograph holding in his right hand? [lulav] What is he holding in his left hand? [etrog] How do you know the boy is not holding a lemon? [An etrog has a stem, called a *pitom*. In the cover picture the *pitom* is at the top of the etrog.] On what holiday do we use these items? [Sukkot]

Have the children look at the illustration of a lulav on the second page of the folder while you teach them the three types of leaves. The tall branch in the middle is from a palm tree. The long, thin leaves on the left are from a willow tree. The small, oval leaves on the right are from a myrtle bush.

Jewish Value
God Is Everywhere

Ask the students whether there is any place where God cannot be found. To emphasize this idea, ask the students if God can be found in their bedroom, the supermarket, the space shuttle, underwater, etc.

What do we do with the lulav on Sukkot? [shake it] In what directions do we shake the lulav? [every direction—north, east, south, west, down, and up] Why do we shake it in these directions? [to show that God is everywhere]

Arts and Crafts

Ask the children to think of their four favorite places. Responses could include locations such as the beach, Disney World, or even their bedroom. Distribute drawing paper and have the children fold it in half. At the top of the first page, have the children write "God Is Everywhere." Then tell them to draw a picture of these places, one on each page.

Hands-On Activities

Have students pretend they are lulavs and shake themselves in all directions.

My Family and Me

Duplicate the "Learning at Home" letter on page 41 of this Guide. Send the letter and folders 10–12 home with the students. Be sure to include the "Family Education Experience" sheet on page 47.

Supplemental Words

leitsan (clown)   lehem (bread)   luah (chalkboard)   lev (heart)

מ
מַצָה

Folder 13

Don't forget to begin the lesson by teaching the new letter and key word. See pages 11–12 for strategies.

Key Word
Matzah
The cracker like unleavened bread eaten on Passover. The Israelites fled Egypt so quickly that their bread dough did not have time to rise.

Let's Talk About It
Briefly review the story of Passover and emphasize the reason that we eat matzah on Passover. Why did the Israelites bring the dough with them? [They did not know how long they would be in the wilderness or where they would get food.] Ask the children how they would feel if someone told them that they had to pack up all their belongings in a hurry and leave their homes.

Jewish Value
The Connection of the Mezuzah to Pesah
Review the story of the Ten Plagues. What did the Israelites have to do to protect their homes from the Angel of Death before the coming of the tenth plague? [spread the blood of the Passover sacrifice on their doorpost] The mezuzah reminds us of how God protected the Israelites at that time and how God will continue to protect our people.

Arts and Crafts
Mix flour and water until it can be kneaded easily. Knead and roll the dough into thin sheets. Punch it with a fork and bake it in an extremely hot oven until slightly brown. Traditionally, for the matzah to be kosher, the entire process must take less than eighteen minutes so that the dough has no chance to rise. Use a timer for fun. Make sure the children understand that the matzah will not come out like the matzah they buy in the store because a standard oven is not hot enough.

Hands-On Activities
Pose this riddle: "What sweet treat do you get if you put two Mems together?" [Mem & Mems— M&M's ®] Then distribute the candies and have the students make a letter Mem with them. If a child has a peanut allergy, he or she should not eat M&M's, even if they are plain chocolate.

My Family and Me
Have a matzah-tasting party with different types of matzahs (e.g., plain, whole wheat, flavored), and various spreads (e.g., butter, jelly, cream cheese). Each family member votes for his or her favorite kind of matzah and spread. You can also say the *Hamotzi* blessing before eating.

Supplemental Words
mezuzah

נ

נֵר תָּמִיד

Folder 14

Don't forget to begin the lesson by teaching the new letter and key word. See pages 11–12 for strategies.

Key Word
Ner Tamid
Eternal light. The light that hangs above the *Aron Kodesh* to remind us that God is always with us.

Let's Talk About It
Where do you see the *ner tamid*? [above the Ark in the synagogue sanctuary] Does the *ner tamid* in your synagogue look like the one in the picture on the first page? Explain that each *ner tamid* looks different but that they will see one in every synagogue. You can also explain that in the past the *ner tamid* was lighted with oil, but now we usually use a light bulb.

Jewish Value
Lighting Shabbat Candles
God created light on the first day of creation. However, that light did not shine from the sun because "the lights in the sky" were not created until the fourth day. If that is the case, where did the light come from? There is a tradition that says the light on the first day came directly from God. When we light Shabbat candles on Friday evening, we welcome God into our homes.

Arts and Crafts
Make Shabbat candlesticks. Give each student a large hunk of clay and two short Shabbat candles. The students should flatten the clay with their hands, to about an inch thick. Have them set their candles firmly into the clay. Then they can decorate their candleholders with paint or by carving Jewish symbols into the clay.

Hands-On Activities
Ask the students to list different occasions when we use candles in Judaism. [Shabbat, holidays, Hanukkah, yahrtzeit (anniversary of the death of a loved one), Havdalah] Bring each of these types of candles to class and discuss how each is different.

My Family and Me
The "Family Education Experience" sheet on page 48, which contains the text and a description of lighting Shabbat candles, should be sent home with the "Learning at Home" letter on page 42 after folders 13–15 are completed. Encourage parents to make lighting Shabbat candles part of their weekly routine.

Supplemental Words
ner (candle)

ס

סֻכָּה

Folder 15

Don't forget to begin the lesson by teaching the new letter and key word. See pages 11–12 for strategies.

Key Word
Sukkah

The sukkah reminds us of the booths that the farmers slept in during harvest time in ancient Israel. It also reminds us of the huts our ancestors lived in during their forty years of wandering.

Let's Talk About It

Ask the students to identify the cover picture. [sukkah] On what holiday do we build a sukkah? [Sukkot] What items are used to decorate the sukkah in the picture? [pumpkins, corn, apples, tree branches, etc.] What do they all have in common? [items from nature] Briefly review the holiday of Sukkot.

Jewish Value

Recognizing God as the Source of Food

Ask the students why they think we decorate the sukkah with fruits and vegetables. Sukkot celebrates the fall harvest, when fruits and vegetables are ready to be picked. By hanging them in the sukkah, we remind ourselves that our food comes from the earth, which is God's creation. Sukkot is the time to thank God for the food that we need in order to live and grow.

Arts and Crafts

Make an edible sukkah. Take four squares of graham crackers and apply a large amount of prepared frosting to the edges of each cracker. Stick them together to form a standing "box" without a front. Apply additional frosting to the roof and sprinkle on some coconut. Add green food coloring to make the roof look like grass or foliage.

Hands-On Activities

Ask each student to bring in one item of nonperishable food to be donated to a food bank. Teach that while we thank God for providing us with food, we must do our part to help those who cannot afford to provide for themselves and their families. Consider having your class sponsor a school-wide food drive.

My Family and Me

Duplicate the "Learning at Home" letter on page 42 of this Guide. Send the letter and folders 13–15 home with the students. Be sure to include the "Family Education Experience" sheet on page 48.

Helpful Hints

When teaching the letter Samech, teach the children that "Samech is like a circle." This will help them to associate the letter name and its shape.

Supplemental Words

sefer (book)   soos (horse)   sevivon (Hanukkah top)

עֵץ

Folder 16

Don't forget to begin the lesson by teaching the new letter and key word. See pages 11–12 for strategies.

Key Word
Etz
Tree

Jewish Value

The Importance of Trees

Trees have always held a special place in Judaism. Trees are so important that the Torah commands Jewish soldiers not to cut down or destroy even the trees of the people they are fighting against. The Torah states: "Do not destroy the trees, because they did nothing to you." Indeed, this verse from Deuteronomy 20:19 is the source for the mitzvah of *bal tash'hit*—protecting the environment.

If you discussed the Jewish value of protecting the environment when the Vav folder was taught, review the concept at this time. If not, refer to page 19 and teach it now. After discussing this mitzvah, ask the students to list things that trees provide for us or for animals. [e.g, fruit, shade, homes to animals, wood]

Arts and Crafts

Build a forest in your classroom. Spread poster paper on the floor across the room. Have each student paint a tree. After the mural has dried, hang it up on the wall. Keep in mind that this can be a very time-consuming project.

Hands-On Activities

Sit on the floor with the class and say: "Pretend that it's spring and everything is waking up after the winter. We are small trees. Raise your hands—not your arms. Our hands are the tiny branches.

"Let's slowly stand up. Now look how we, as trees, are growing. Let's stand with our feet apart. Now look at our feet. They are the roots that keep the trees from falling over.

"Let's stretch our arms and hands upward. See how a tree grows up and up and up. Is this as high as you can reach? Will you be able to reach higher next year? How long do you think it takes a tree to grow as big as you are? It takes many years for different trees to give us fruit, shade, and wood."

My Family and Me

Teach the word *oogah* and encourage the students to make cupcakes with their families and decorate them with letters of the Alef Bet, using tubes of frosting.

Supplemental Words

oogah (cake)

פ

פַּרְפַּר

Folder 17

 Don't forget to begin the lesson by teaching the new letter and key word. See pages 11–12 for strategies.

Key Word
Parpar
Butterfly

Jewish Value
We Can Always Change and Improve Ourselves
A butterfly begins its life in an entirely different form, as a caterpillar. Then it is transformed into a chrysalis and, after two to three weeks, emerges remade into a beautiful butterfly.

Can people transform themselves? We are constantly changing things about ourselves—the way we look, the way we think, the way we act, the things we like, how we treat people. Some people may change the way they eat entirely so that their diet is healthier. Others may decide to wear nicer clothes. Perhaps you want to make an effort to watch less television and to spend more time reading books. Every year on Yom Kippur we look at ourselves and the ways in which we have behaved in the past year. We think of ways in which we can improve and be better people in the coming year.

Hands-On Activities
Have the children pretend they are caterpillars coming out of their cocoons and suddenly realizing that they have turned into butterflies.

My Family and Me
Have a family discussion about how each of us can do something to transform and improve ourselves. All family members should choose one area that they can work on to improve themselves.

Helpful Hints
When teaching the sound of the letter Pay, have the children imitate the sound of popcorn popping.

Supplemental Words
parah (cow)   pa'amon (bell)   pil (elephant)

צ

צְדָקָה

Folder 18

just a **Reminder** Don't forget to begin the lesson by teaching the new letter and key word. See pages 11–12 for strategies.

Key Word
Tsedakah

Justice or righteousness. It is most often used to refer to financial assistance to the poor.

Jewish Value
Tsedakah

Ask whether anyone recognizes the word *tsedakah* and knows what it means. Emphasize that tsedakah not only refers to giving money, but also means helping people in areas related to monetary issues. Give several examples (e.g., giving someone a job, collecting food for the homeless). Then help the students brainstorm more examples of tsedakah.

Explain that tsedakah means "justice." While this word may be too complex for the students, point out that the word *justice* begins with the word *just*. This teaches us that we do acts of tsedakah because it is the just or right thing to do. We are commanded by God to do acts of tsedakah. All Jews, no matter how rich or poor, famous or not famous, should try to fulfill the mitzvah of tsedakah.

Arts and Crafts

Have each student bring in a container with a plastic lid, such as a coffee can, to use in making a tsedakah box. Cut a coin slot in the lid. Make construction paper available to wrap around the container. The students should decorate the construction paper with Jewish symbols and pictures. Then have the students glue the construction paper onto the containers. Bring enough coins so that you can deposit one into each student's tsedakah box.

My Family and Me

(A) Every Friday, before Shabbat, family members can put change into a tsedakah box. When the box is full, the family can meet to decide where to donate the money.

(B) Duplicate the "Learning at Home" letter on page 43 of this Guide. Send the letter and folders 16–18 home with the students.

Helpful Hints

When teaching Tsadee, ask students for English words that have the "TS" sound. [e.g., pizza, boats]

Supplemental Words

ts'fardeya (frog)

ק

קֶשֶׁת

Folder 19

Don't forget to begin the lesson by teaching the new letter and key word. See pages 11–12 for strategies.

Key Word
Keshet
Rainbow

Jewish Value

The Rainbow as a Promise from God

Ask the students: "Who has seen a rainbow? When did you see the rainbow? Which colors are in a rainbow?" You can help the children remember the colors of the rainbow by teaching them the mnemonic "**Roy G Biv**"—**r**ed, **o**range, **y**ellow, **g**reen, **b**lue, **i**ndigo, **v**iolet. Ask whether anyone knows a Bible story about a rainbow. Then, tell the story of Noah and the flood. Emphasize the ending of the story, which says that the rainbow is a reminder from God that God will never again destroy the world.

Arts and Crafts

Give each student a large piece of white drawing paper. Have students draw a picture of an outdoor scene using crayons, and make sure that a rainbow is a prominent part of the scene. For best results, they should press hard on the crayons while drawing. Dilute various colors of tempera paints by adding equal amounts of water to cups of the paint. Brush diluted paint over the paper, completely covering the picture. The crayons will resist the paint, thus creating an interesting effect.

Hands-On Activities

Make a rainbow in your classroom. If you have windows in your room, obtain a prism and hold it up to the sunlight to make a rainbow on the classroom wall. You can also make a rainbow by letting sunlight reflect off a pot of water.

My Family and Me

The *keshet* was God's promise to never again destroy the world. Suggest to the students that they discuss with their family members promises that they can make to each other.

Supplemental Words

Kiddush   kof (monkey)

ר

רִמּוֹנִים

Folder 20

Don't forget to begin the lesson by teaching the new letter and key word. See pages 11–12 for strategies.

Key Word
Rimonim
Bells; special ornaments for the Torah

Jewish Value
Hiddur Mitzvah
When we value something, we often decorate it. For example, we decorate our rooms, homes, books, and other things. In the same way, we dress the Torah in a beautiful mantle, *rimonim*, and a breastplate. Can you think of other Jewish objects that we try to make as decorative and as beautiful as possible? [e.g, mezuzah, Kiddush cup, hallah cover] In Judaism, there is a concept known as *hiddur mitzvah*—beautifying or enhancing a mitzvah. This means that we want to make each mitzvah as special as possible. For example, we don't use a paper cup to make Kiddush, but instead use a special Kiddush cup.

Arts and Crafts
Beautifying the classroom with children's artwork is also part of *hiddur mitzvah*. After all, *Talmud Torah*—the study of Torah and Jewish subjects—is one of the most important *mitzvot*. Allow students to choose one Jewish object and then draw a picture of it using crayons or colored pencils. Tell them to make it especially beautiful! Afterward, decorate the classroom walls with the artwork to fulfill the mitzvah of *hiddur mitzvah*.

Hands-On Activities
Take a trip to the sanctuary and remove a Torah from the *Aron Kodesh*. Undress the Torah, showing and explaining each item to the students. Allow the students to see the Torah close up, and explain that a Torah is written by hand. Tell the students that we do not touch the parchment of the Torah with our hands because we do not want to smudge the words or get them dirty. Make sure the students see the Hebrew text, and ask them to say a Hebrew letter that they see and recognize. Tell the children in advance that the letters in the Torah will not look exactly the same as the letters in their folders. The letters in the Torah are fancier, more decorative, and more elaborate. For example, point out letters that are decorated with crowns on them.

My Family and Me
Encourage families to discuss ways that they can enhance and beautify the observance of *mitzvot* in their homes. Ideas could include buying more beautiful Jewish ceremonial objects, setting the table more festively for Shabbat or holiday dinners, and so on.

Supplemental Words
rakevet (train)

שׁ

שׁוֹפָר

Folder 21

 Don't forget to begin the lesson by teaching the new letter and key word. See pages 11–12 for strategies.

Key Word
Shofar
The horn of a male sheep. The shofar is blown on Rosh Hashanah and at the conclusion of Yom Kippur.

Jewish Value
Shofar
On which holidays do we hear the shofar blown? [Rosh Hashanah and at the end of Yom Kippur] How do you feel when you hear the shofar? What do you think of when you hear the shofar? There are many reasons given for why the shofar is sounded, but here are two reasons to share with the students: (1) The sound of the shofar gets our attention and reminds us that we have to behave in the ways that God wants of us. (2) Just as a trumpet is often blown to introduce a king or queen or the leader of a country, so the shofar introduces God.

Arts and Crafts
Cut out a shofar shape from a paper plate. Turn the shape over and trace it on another paper plate. Cut it out. Place the two shapes together to form a shofar. Punch holes along the two sides and sew together with yarn. Tie a knot at each end. Depending upon the ability of your students, you may want to prepare this project before class and have the children do only the sewing.

Hands-On Activities
Invite a guest to come into the classroom and demonstrate how a shofar is blown. Tell the children to listen carefully to the sounds of the shofar, and ask them how each sound makes them feel.

My Family and Me
A family member should review the "In School or At Home" exercise with the child and then encourage the child to make up more riddles.

Helpful Hints
When teaching the sound of the Shin, ask the students to make its sound. As the room fills with the sound SSSSSSHHHH, you might joke that you don't want to be quiet!

Supplemental Words
shemesh (sun)   shulhan (table)   sha'on (clock)   Shabbat

34

ת
תּוֹרָה

Folder 22

Don't forget to begin the lesson by teaching the new letter and key word. See pages 11–12 for strategies.

Key Word
Torah
The Torah comprises the first five books of the Bible. It is also known as the Five Books of Moses.

Jewish Value
The Importance of Torah
Why is the Torah so important to the Jewish people? [It contains the stories of the origins of the Jewish people, as well as the *mitzvot* we follow to live a Jewish life.] What would happen if Jews stopped studying Torah? [People would not know what it means to be Jewish and how to live Jewishly. Soon there would be no more Jews left.] Relate the following saying of Rabbi Akiba and discuss what it means: *Just as fish cannot live without water, so Jews cannot live without Torah.*

Hands-On Activities
Ask students, one by one, to name one or two things that they have learned during the year in religious school. Explain that every time they learn something about Judaism, they are fulfilling the mitzvah of Talmud Torah—the study of Torah. List on the chalkboard what everyone has said. At the end comment on how many things have been learned over the course of the year.

My Family and Me
(A) Encourage families to take a little time each week to engage in Talmud Torah. This could be something as simple as having a family discussion each Friday night about something that one of the children has learned in religious school.

(B) Duplicate the "Learning at Home" letter on page 44 of this Guide. Send the letter and folders 19–22 home with the students.

Helpful Hints
When teaching the Tav, show the children that "Tav has a toe" (at bottom left). How does the Tav differ from the Het?

Supplemental Words
tapoo'ah (apple)

Review Folder

Folder 23

Jewish Values

Siyum Hasefer (Completing the Book)

Each year we finish reading our most important book, the Torah, and immediately begin reading it again. At this time we have a large celebration called *Simhat Torah*. Traditionally, we have smaller celebrations when we finish studying other Jewish books or when we complete a course of Jewish study. Such a celebration is called a *siyum hasefer*.

When the class has finished *Let's Discover the Alef Bet*, it is time for a celebration. Include the students in planning the *siyum hasefer* so that they will feel that it is their celebration. Following are some appropriate activities for such a celebration:

- Invite the Rabbi, Cantor, Education Director, and parents.
- Do a formal reading of the cover page of the Review folder (the entire Alef Bet).
- Recite the *sheheheyanu* prayer.
- Serve refreshments accompanied by the appropriate blessings.
- Sing "Hatikvah" and other Hebrew songs.
- Present a certificate of completion to each student. (See the back page of the folder.)

Arts and Crafts

Have a variety of arts and crafts materials available and let the students make decorations for the *siyum hasefer* celebration.

Hands-On Activities

Before class, draw each Hebrew letter on a sheet of construction paper. Punch holes in the top of the sheets and tie pieces of yarn through them so that the students can wear them around their necks. Allow each student to choose one letter and then decorate it. When finished, have students parade around the room wearing their Hebrew letters. When they reach your desk, they should tell you the name and sound of their letter.

My Family and Me

Encourage families to continue the *siyum hasefer* celebration at home by having a special dinner in honor of the occasion. Perhaps the student's favorite food can be served.

PART 2

LEARNING AT HOME

LEARNING AT HOME
Folders 1–3

Dear Parent,

Your child has begun the exciting process of learning the Hebrew alphabet. So far we have learned the first three letters—Alef, Bet, and Gimmel. We have also learned several Hebrew words and discussed important Jewish values. Show your child that you value his or her Hebrew studies by reading through these folders and asking questions about the material that has been covered.

Here are some things you can do at home to enhance your child's learning of the Hebrew alphabet.

❶ Reviewing the Folders

Folder 1 introduces Alef—the first letter of the Hebrew alphabet—and the phrase *Alef Bet* as the name of the Hebrew alphabet. Ask your child to point out the Alef to you on the Alef Bet chart that is on the front page of Folder 1. Also don't forget to ask in which direction we read Hebrew!

Folder 2 presents the letter Bet and the word *bayit*—house. We also learned *beit knesset*—synagogue. We hope that your child will feel as comfortable in the *beit knesset* as in your *bayit*. Think about how you can help your child to feel this level of comfort in the synagogue.

Folder 3 introduces the letter Gimmel and the word *glidah*—ice cream. We also learned several other Hebrew words beginning with a Gimmel. Have your child point out the words in the folder that are related to food.

❷ Treasure Hunt

Go on a treasure hunt in your *bayit*—your home. Look for as many Jewish objects as you can find. These might include *kippot* (yarmulkes), *mezuzot*, a Hanukkah menorah, etc. Then discuss with your child what you feel makes your home Jewish.

LEARNING AT HOME

Folders 4–6

Dear Parent,

Your child's introduction to the Hebrew language has continued with the letters Dalet, Hay, and Vav. We have also discussed such diverse ideas as flag waving, concluding Shabbat, and the beauty of a rose.

Here are some things you can do at home to enhance your child's learning of the Hebrew alphabet.

❶ Reviewing the Folders

In Folder 4 the children learned the letter Dalet and the Hebrew word *degel*—flag. In the folder are pictures of the flag of Israel. Ask your child what colors are on an Israeli flag and what symbol is in the middle. If you have ever traveled to Israel, share some stories about that trip with your child.

Folder 5 introduces the letter Hay, as well as the words *Havdalah* and *Haggadah.* We discussed the different components of the Havdalah ceremony, which concludes Shabbat, and the important purpose of a Haggadah at a Passover seder.

Folder 6 presents the letter Vav and the word *vered*—rose. Make sure to have your child ask you the riddle found on the second page of the folder.

❷ Making Havdalah

The Havdalah ceremony, which marks the conclusion of Shabbat, is among the most unique rituals in Judaism and can be a moving experience for the entire family. A special characteristic of Havdalah is that there are roles for several family members as part of the ceremony. These roles include holding the candle, the spice box, and the Kiddush cup. It is nice to follow Havdalah by doing something together as a family.

LEARNING AT HOME

Folders 7–9

Dear Parent,

   The children are becoming increasingly comfortable with Hebrew as we learn more and more Hebrew letters and words.

   Don't forget to review the "In School and At Home" exercises with your child. Here are some additional things you can do at home to enhance your child's learning of the Hebrew alphabet.

❶ Reviewing the Folders

The focus of Folder 7 is the letter Zayin and the word *zebrah* (pronounced Zeh-BRAH in Hebrew). The Hebrew language has numerous words that sound similar to English words. Ask your child what the prevailing opinion of the class was to the question, "Do you think a zebra is white with black stripes, or black with white stripes?"

Folder 8 introduces the letter Het, as well as the words *hallah* and *Hanukkah.* As a special treat, make French toast from hallah. The third page of the folder contains the directions for playing the dreidel game. Ask your child which two letters that have been learned so far are found on a dreidel.

Folder 9 presents the letter Tet and the word *tallit.* If you have a tallit in the house, you can take this opportunity to show it to your child and explain when you received it. Perhaps it was when you became a Bar or Bat Mitzvah, or another special occasion. We also read about the holiday of Tu B'Shevat. Have your child tell you something about the way that this holiday can be celebrated.

❷ Hamotzi—The Blessing for Bread

You will find the blessing over bread written in Hebrew, in English, and in transliteration on the back page of Folder 8. We learned it in conjunction with learning the letter Het and the word *hallah.* Practice saying the blessing with your child, and take the opportunity to recite it when your family eats Friday night dinner. Beginning with a blessing sets a pleasing tone for the meal.

LEARNING AT HOME
Folders 10–12

Dear Parent,

Folder 11 marked the halfway point in our study of the Hebrew alphabet. Please continue to support your child by showing an interest in the material that we have been covering.

Here are some things you can do at home to enhance your child's learning of the Hebrew alphabet.

❶ Reviewing the Folders

In Folder 10 we learned the letter Yud and the words *yeladim* (children) and *yad* (hand). On the back page of the folder is a picture dictionary of the key Hebrew words learned so far. Look at this page with your child and say the Hebrew word for each picture. Then ask your child to identify the name and the sound of the first letter of each word.

Folder 11 introduces the letter Kaf and the words *kelev* (dog) and *kippah* (yarmulke). You can use the word *kelev* as a jumping-off point to discuss the ways that we should treat animals. In Judaism, this is known as the mitzvah of *tsa'ar ba'alei hayyim*—being kind to animals.

Folder 12 focuses on the letter Lamed and the word *lulav*. Ask your child on which holiday we shake a lulav, in what directions, and why.

❷ Parental Blessing over Children

In Folder 10 your child learned the words *yeladim* and *yad*. Judaism provides a very special opportunity for parents to put their *yadayim* (plural of *yad*) on their *yeladim*. Traditionally, parents bless their children before reciting Kiddush on Friday night. This can create a uniquely close and tender moment between you and your child as you place your hands on his or her head and say the blessing. The recitation of this blessing is a very special way you can express your love for your child.

LEARNING AT HOME

Folders 13–15

Dear Parent,

    The key words learned in these three folders—*matzah, ner tamid,* and *sukkah*—are all linked to Jewish ritual. From these words, we see the inextricable connection between the Hebrew language and Jewish tradition.

    Here are some things you can do at home to enhance your child's learning of the Hebrew alphabet.

❶ Reviewing the Folders

Folder 13 introduces the letter Mem and the words *matzah* and *mezuzah.* Something fun to do at home is to have a matzah-tasting party. Buy different types of matzahs (e.g., plain, whole wheat, flavored) and various spreads (e.g., butter, jelly, cream cheese). Have each family member vote on his or her favorite kind of matzah and spread. You can also say the *Hamotzi* blessing before eating!

In Folder 14 we learned the letter Nun. We also studied the word *ner* (candle) and the term *ner tamid* (eternal light). Make sure to play the "computer game" on the back page of the folder. Children enjoy it, and it is great reinforcement for the names and shapes of the Hebrew letters.

Folder 15, which presents the letter Samech, concentrates on the words *sukkah* and *Sukkot.* Ask your child what the difference is between these two similar words.

❷ Lighting Shabbat Candles

In Folder 14 your child learned the word *ner*—candle. Lighting candles to welcome Shabbat casts a warm glow over the household. Gather the entire family for candlelighting and then wish each other a Shabbat Shalom.

> *Baruch atah, Adonai Eloheinu, melech ha'olam, asher kidshanu b'mitzvotav v'tzivanu l'hadlik ner shel Shabbat.*

> Blessed are You, Adonai our God, Ruler of the world, who makes us holy with *mitzvot* and commands us to kindle the Sabbath lights.

LEARNING AT HOME
Folders 16–18

Dear Parent,

The children have recently learned the letters Ayin, Pay, and Tsadee. In these folders we studied words that relate to improving ourselves and the world in which we live.

Here are some things you can do at home to enhance your child's learning of the Hebrew alphabet.

❶ Reviewing the Folders

In Folder 16 we taught the letter Ayin, as well as the words *etz* (tree) and *oogah* (cake). Consider making cupcakes with your child and decorating them with letters of the Alef Bet, using tubes of frosting. Although we have not been teaching the children how to write the letters, you can approximate their shapes by copying them from the folders or from the Alef Bet chart.

Folder 17 introduces the letter Pay and the word *parpar* (butterfly). You can have a revealing discussion with your child about ways in which we can change ourselves, just as a caterpillar changes into a butterfly. We can change the way we look, the way we think, the way we act, and so on. At dinner one night have a family discussion about this idea, and ask family members to choose one area that they can work on to improve themselves.

Folder 18 teaches the letter Tsadee and the words *ts'fardeya* (frog) and *tsedakah*. These two words exemplify that Hebrew is a modern, vibrant language consisting of words for everyday life as well as traditional Jewish terminology.

❷ Making Tsedakah a Habit

If your child did not make a tsedakah box in class during the study of Folder 18, you can help him or her make one at home. Make it routine that every Friday, before Shabbat, family members put change into the tsedakah box. When it is full, the family can meet and decide where to donate the money.

LEARNING AT HOME

Folders 19–22

Dear Parent,

We are very excited to have learned all 22 letters of the Alef Bet, as well as a variety of Hebrew words. Celebrate and show pride in your child's accomplishment.

Although we have completed our course of study, you can continue to do things at home to enhance your child's learning of the Hebrew alphabet.

❶ Reviewing the Folders

Folder 19 tells us about the letter Koof and the words *keshet* (rainbow) and *Kiddush.* Discuss with your child the story of Noah, as well as God's use of the rainbow as a symbol of the promise never again to destroy the world. What promises can family members make to each other?

Folder 20 presents the letter Resh and the words *rimonim* (Torah headpiece) and *rakevet* (train). *Rimonim* adorn and beautify the Torah. Think about ways in which you can enhance and beautify the celebration of Judaism in your home.

In Folder 21 we learned the letter Shin and the words *shofar* and *shemesh* (sun). Review the "In School or At Home" activity on the back page of the folder, and then have your child make up more riddles to ask you.

The final folder—22—introduces the letter Tav and the word *Torah.* Perhaps it is fitting that this word concludes your child's study of Hebrew, since there is a traditional saying that the study of Torah equals all of God's other commandments.

❷ Talmud Torah at the Table

Talmud Torah refers not only to the study of Torah itself, but more generally to the study and discussion of anything related to Judaism. Take some time each week to engage in Talmud Torah as a family. This could be as simple as asking your children at dinner to talk about what they have learned in religious school.

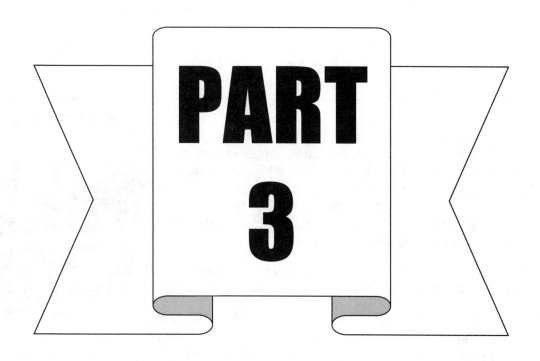

PART
3

FAMILY
EDUCATION
EXPERIENCE

Family Education Experience

Concluding Shabbat with Havdalah

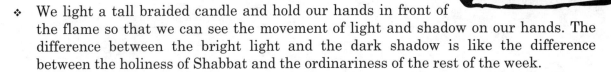

When three stars appear in the Saturday evening sky, it is time for Havdalah, the beautiful ceremony that separates Shabbat from the rest of the week. We recite a blessing before each of the following parts of the Havdalah ceremony:

❖ Just as we began Shabbat by reciting Kiddush, we also end Shabbat with the blessing over wine or grape juice.

❖ We smell sweet spices, hoping that the aroma of Shabbat, symbolized by the spices, will follow us into the new week.

❖ We light a tall braided candle and hold our hands in front of the flame so that we can see the movement of light and shadow on our hands. The difference between the bright light and the dark shadow is like the difference between the holiness of Shabbat and the ordinariness of the rest of the week.

Havdalah, which means "separation," celebrates the separation between the holy and the ordinary. At the conclusion of Havdalah some people extinguish the candle by dipping it into the wine. Then we wish our family and friends *shavua tov*—a good week!

Following are the four central blessings of Havdalah. The complete text of the Havdalah ceremony can be found in most prayerbooks.

Blessing over wine or grape juice:

בָּרוּךְ אַתָּה, ה' אֱלֹהֵינוּ, מֶלֶךְ הָעוֹלָם, בּוֹרֵא פְּרִי הַגָּפֶן.

Baruch atah, Adonai Eloheinu, melech ha'olam, borei p'ri hagafen.

Praised are You, Adonai our God, Ruler of the world, who creates the fruit of the vine.

Blessing over spices:

בָּרוּךְ אַתָּה, ה' אֱלֹהֵינוּ, מֶלֶךְ הָעוֹלָם, בּוֹרֵא מִינֵי בְשָׂמִים.

Baruch atah, Adonai Eloheinu, melech ha'olam, borei minei v'samim.

Praised are You, Adonai our God, Ruler of the world, who creates all kinds of spices.

Blessing over flame of the Havdalah candle:

בָּרוּךְ אַתָּה, ה' אֱלֹהֵינוּ, מֶלֶךְ הָעוֹלָם, בּוֹרֵא מְאוֹרֵי הָאֵשׁ.

Baruch atah, Adonai Eloheinu, melech ha'olam, borei m'orei ha'eish.

Praised are You, Adonai our God, Ruler of the world, who creates the light of fire.

Blessing of separation:

בָּרוּךְ אַתָּה, ה',הַמַּבְדִּיל בֵּין קֹדֶשׁ לְחוֹל.

Baruch atah, Adonai, hamavdil bein kodesh l'hol.

Praised are You, Adonai, who separates the holy from the ordinary.

Family Education Experience

Blessing Your Children

Blessing your children can be a uniquely intimate moment. Through the gentle touch of your hands and the sound of your voice, your children will feel your love for them and your hopes for their future. Before the recitation of the Kiddush, each child is blessed individually and in descending order of age. Place your hands on your child's head and recite the following blessing:

For sons:

יְשִׂמְךָ אֱלֹהִים כְּאֶפְרַיִם וְכִמְנַשֶּׁה.

Y'simcha Elohim k'efrayim v'chi'menashe.

May God make you as Ephraim and Mennasseh.

For daughters:

יְשִׂמֵךְ אֱלֹהִים כְּשָׂרָה, רִבְקָה, רָחֵל וְלֵאָה.

Y'simech Elohim k'sara, rivka, rahel v'leah.

May God make you as Sarah, Rebecca, Rachel, and Leah.

For all children, conclude with the following:

יְבָרֶכְךָ ה׳ וְיִשְׁמְרֶךָ.
יָאֵר ה׳ פָּנָיו אֵלֶיךָ וִיחֻנֶּךָּ.
יִשָּׂא ה׳ פָּנָיו אֵלֶיךָ וְיָשֵׂם לְךָ שָׁלוֹם.

Y'varech'cha Adonai v'yishm'recha.
Ya'er Adonai panav eilecha vihuneka.
Yisa Adonai panav eilecha v'yasem l'cha shalom.

May Adonai bless you and guard you.
May Adonai show you favor and be gracious to you.
May Adonai show you kindness and grant you peace.

You may add your own words as well. Make this moment of religious communication between you and your child personal and special.

Lighting Shabbat Candles

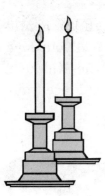

The Sabbath is ushered into the Jewish home when Shabbat candles are kindled and blessed. According to custom, at least two candles must be lit. The two candles represent the commandments in the Torah—to "remember" and to "observe" the Sabbath day. Some hold the tradition of lighting one candle for each member of the family. Practice saying the blessing with your child, and try to make it a regular activity to light the Shabbat candles together on Friday evening.

1) Light the candles.

2) Move your hands around the flames several times and bring them toward your face. This gesture symbolically welcomes the Sabbath into your home.

3) Place your hands over your eyes, so that you will not see the Sabbath lights until after you have recited the blessing:

בָּרוּךְ אַתָּה, ה' אֱלֹהֵינוּ, מֶלֶךְ הָעוֹלָם, אֲשֶׁר קִדְּשָׁנוּ בְּמִצְוֹתָיו וְצִוָּנוּ לְהַדְלִיק נֵר שֶׁל שַׁבָּת.

Baruch atah, Adonai Eloheinu, melech ha'olam, asher kidshanu b'mitzvotav v'tzivanu l'hadlik ner shel Shabbat.

Blessed are You, Adonai our God, Ruler of the world, who makes us holy with *mitzvot* and commands us to kindle the Sabbath lights.

4) Take another moment to recite a personal prayer for those you love.

5) Remove your hands from your face and open your eyes.

Shabbat has arrived in your home. Wish each other Shabbat Shalom, a peaceful Shabbat.